Beaded Images II

Intricate Beaded Jewelry Using Brick Stitch

Written & Illustrated by:
Barbara Elbe

Eagle's View Publishing Company
6756 North Fork Road
Liberty, UT 84310

IBSN: 0-943604-49-4
Library of Congress Catalog Card Number 95-61193

FIRST EDITION

Elbe, Barbara, 1945-
    Beaded Images II/by Barbara Elbe --
    p,cm,
    ISBN 0-943604-49-4

1. Beadwork. 2. Earrings. 3. Jewelry Making. I. Title.

TT860   745.5942
                                                QB190-277

10 9 8 7 6 5 4 3 2 1

Table Of Contents

Table of Contents

Introduction

Keeping with the tradition of *Beaded Images*, all the original patterns in this book explore the many shapes into which beads can be sculptured. The use of smaller beads is important for detailed work. Delica (DB) beads have been used primarily. There are a few patterns that use Hexagon (HEX) beads. Smaller, #14 size seed beads can be substituted. The majority of patterns are without fringe as their sculptured design and subject matter render it unnecessary.

Under Basic Information there is a listing of abbreviations and terms often used in beading. Each design in the book is coded for level of difficulty. There are five levels in all ranging from * easiest, to ***** most difficult.

Standard instructions for beading and the essentials needed to do sculptured design, increasing and decreasing, are in Chapter One. Because sculptured designs are very difficult to explain, a system of symbols has been used. This is shown with a chart on Page 20.

Chapter Two has quite a variety of patterns, all with horizontal BASE ROWS. They range from a penguin hanging by it's beak , flying mallard ducks, a horse rearing on it's hind legs and a cluster of grapes.

The next chapter is made up of vertical BASE ROW designs. This chapter is filled with cuddly cats, a big eared dog and a yellow ducky that looks vaguely familiar.

Chapter Four, Girls, Curls & Clowns, is just that. There is a girl with lots and lots of blonde, curly, three dimensional hair and a classy lady with a big hat. Clowns with big, red, three dimensional noses round off the book. There is one with a bow tie and orange, curly, three dimensional hair. Another clown is a sad-faced hobo, and last the wild hair clown. All the curls and hair are fully explained.

This is a detailed, well thought out book for the person who likes to explore new creative ideas and techniques.

NOTES

Basic Information

Beads

While the designs in this book can be made with size #14 to #15 seed beads, they can also be made with Delica Beads (DB) or Hexagon Beads (HEX), as pictured in this book.

Delica Beads are about the size of #14 seed beads, Hexagon about the size of #15's. Unlike the round shape of a seed bead, DB and HEX are shaped more like a cylinder or very small bugle. This helps them to fit together snugly like miniature tiles. Completed work will not shift. Also, unlike the seed bead, their holes are very large for their size making them very easy to work with. They are much lighter in weight than seed beads of the same size making the completed earring less heavy. DB and HEX beads are not interchangeable in the main part of a design. Their size and shape are just different enough to cause warpage when used together. They can be interchanged, though, in the fringe.

Seed   DB   HEX

Color wise, DB beads come in over 300 choices. Some of the color changes are so subtle they could be an artist's palette. They come in a variety of coatings that make them shine richly.

A.B. (Aurora Borealis) - A rainbow coating on transparent glass.

Lined - Clear on the outside, color on the inside.

Iris - A rainbow coating on opaque glass.

Luster - A colorless transparent coating that gives a very high gloss.

Matte - A dull appearance on opaque glass; a frosted translucent appearance on transparent glass.

Metallic - Opaque coating that includes gunmetal, bronze, gold, & silver, giving a metallic look.

Opaque - Solid in color allowing no light to pass through.

Pearl, Ceylon - Opaque to translucent pearl-like coating.

Silver/Lined (S/L) - A mirrored effect coming from center of bead.

Transparent - Allows light to pass through, clear or colored bead.

2 Cut - Cut or molded side facets adding sparkle.

HEX beads also come in a large variety of colors and surface coatings, but they don't seem to have the richness DB's have. Many of the opaque colors can be purchased in hanks, making them more affordable. The more exotic colors are sold by the gram.

Hank - Usually consists of 12 strands of beads grouped together, each strand measuring approximately 12 inches in length.

Gram , (g) - 28 grams to an ounce - Both DB & HEX can be purchased by the gram: 5, 10, or 100, and by the kilo.

Kilo, (kg.) - kilogram, 1000 grams - Or a fraction, thereof.

Other beads used in this book:

Austrian Crystal - Made from a high lead-content glass, the consistent facets have highly polished plane surfaces and sharp angles which create brilliance and sparkle.

Druks - Smooth round glass beads. They come in every clear color imaginable as well as AB and opaque colors.

The little 2" x 2" E-Z Grip™ reclosable plastic bags work well for storing beads. Also Plano™ fishing tackle boxes, which come in a variety of sizes, shapes, and styles, are perfect for storage, keeping everything organized.

Needles

The type of needles used for beading are very thin, have small eyes, and are very flexible. They range from size #10, thickest, to #16, thinnest. There are two types, English and Japanese. Because the holes are so large on DB and HEX beads, the somewhat larger, size #12 English needle can be used. It is easier to handle, doesn't bend out of shape as fast, and is easier to thread. Only when the needle will not go through the bead, usually because it has been gone through a number of times and has too much thread in it, is it necessary to switch to a thinner #15 needle. A thinner needle is also needed when using seed beads. Never force a needle through any bead, as it can break the bead and ruin the work.

Thread

The thread used for beading DB and HEX beads is the same used for seed beads. It is a nylon fiber thread called NYMO™. It comes in mainly white and black; although, it does come in some colors on bobbin-size spools. It comes in a variety of sizes (weights). Use size 0 with HEX beads as it is heavier. HEX beads quite often have sharp edges that can slowly wear the thread when making a larger design. The thicker thread holds up better allowing one whole section of thread to be used for one complete design. Use size 00, a thinner thread, for DB beads which are usually smooth around the top edges and don't cause damage to the thread. Other than these reasons, it is a matter of preference as to what weight is chosen. DB and HEX beads have very large holes for their size compared to size #10 or #11 seed beads, so any size thread would work. The smaller #14 and #15 seed beads have extremely small holes, so the thinner size 0 thread would be a better choice. KEVLAR™ is another choice. It is the thread used for making bullet proof vests and is very thin and very strong. It is less likely to stretch than other nylon threads, but it will fray like NYMO™ when run through sharp-edged beads repeatedly. It comes on 50 yard spools, most commonly in beige and black, in a size similar to size 0; although, it can be found in a few colors. KEVLAR™ is priced considerably higher than NYMO™.

Wax

Run the thread across a little 1 1/2" chunk of *beeswax*. This allows the thread to slide through the beadwork with less friction causing less damage to the thread. It also helps to keep the thread from tangling as much.

Workspace

A beading board can be very useful. One can be purchased from a bead supply store or catalog. They are usually made of wood or plastic and come in a variety of sizes. One 6" x 18" x 1" thick works well. This size is big enough to hold all the beads and other items needed for a project. The board keeps everything together so that it can all be picked up at one time and put away. Because the wooden boards have smooth surfaces on which beads tend to roll out of control, a small piece of light colored cloth glued to a piece of cardboard and fitted into a section of the board works well. This gives a nice surface on which to spread the beads out without having to chase them all over the place. The plastic boards are usually felt covered. Next to the board have a small container in which all the *reject* beads can be put. There can be many at times.

Lighting

Good lighting in the workspace is *very important.* Natural lighting is the best. Artificial light reflects off the beads making it hard to tell their color, size or shape. If artificial lighting has to be used, fluorescent seems to be the most natural.

Chapter One
Getting Started

1. Cut a length of thread approximately 1 1/2 to 3 yards in length depending on the type and size of the design. Each pattern gives the exact length of thread to use and the exact location on the thread to place the needle.

2. Wax the length of thread with beeswax running it across the surface two or three times.

   The thread on a bobbin-size spool comes off in small spirals and is difficult to use, as it tangles easily in this condition. If the thread is run through wet fingers then stretched, the spirals lessen considerably. This is usually done before waxing.

3. Next position the needle, using the #12 English, where instructed for each pattern. This is approximately midway on the first third of the thread for the top half of the design, usually leaving two thirds for the bottom half and the fringe. When the design does not have fringe, the thread is divided more equally.

4. Consistency in the selection of beads is very important. Most beads of the same size and type are consistent in their width but not their height (See Insert, Page 7). As a row of beads is being worked, each time a new bead is being added to the design, hold it up on the needle next to the previously strung bead and compare it in size before adding it to the design.

   Keep a relaxed tension on the thread. If the thread is pulled too tight when making the design, the earring becomes very rigid and develops ripples. A rigid earring can sometimes seem more desirable, but it is not worth the distortion it can cause.

Main Section of Earring

1. **ROW ONE - BASE ROW**: Usually the middle or widest point of a design unless otherwise specified. Everything is worked off of this row.

   Pick up two beads with the needle and position them just past the end of the double section of thread. Holding them in place with the thumb and forefinger, bring the needle around and go back through them in same direction making a circle. (Figure #1)

   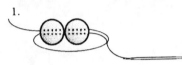

2. Pull the circle up tight positioning the two beads side by side. (Figure #2)

3. Continue adding beads until the desired amount for the base row is made. (Figure #3) Turn the work around. All work is done from left to right.

   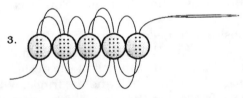

4. **SECOND ROW**: Now working backwards over the row just completed, with a bead on the thread, bring the needle through the top loop that goes between the last two beads of the first row. (Figure #4) Pull the bead into place.

   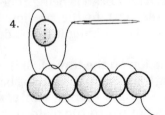

5. Bring the needle back up through the bead, coming up through the bottom, and pull it down. (Figure #5)

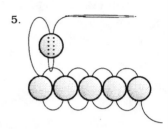

   If the thread is pulled too tight, the work will become very rigid and many times will warp. Try to relax, just pull up slack without yanking. The completed work will be more flexible and smoother to the touch. This is very important.

6. Add beads, in the same fashion as just explained, to the end of the row. (Figure #6) Turn the work around.

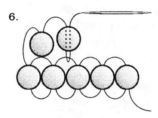

7. Continue in the same way (Figure #7) until there is a row of just 2 beads. Turn the work so that the thread comes out of the bead on the left. (Figure #8)

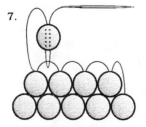
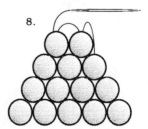

8. At this point the loop that holds the ear wire is made. Add 4 beads along with the ear wire to the thread. Go down through the right bead on the top row and up through the left one. Pull this down to form a loop. Go through these beads and ear wire 2 - 3 times to add strength to the loop (Figure #9) ending up on the right side.

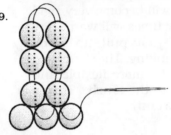

9.

9. The top part of the earring is now complete and it is time to tie off the thread. Make the knots on the outer threads of the earring (Figure #10). Go through the outer thread with the needle far enough to form a small loop. Go through that loop with the needle and then pull down. Repeat. A knot is now formed. This is the same kind of knot used in hand sewing.

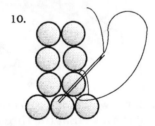

10.

10. Pull the knot down through the bead closest to the knot (Figure #11) until it can no longer be seen. Run the needle through 4 to 6 more beads so there is a section of thread after the knot before cutting. Cut close to the work with a small pair of scissors or clippers. Be careful not to cut any other thread.

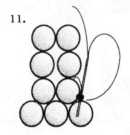

11.

11. Move the needle to the other section of thread and start the lower part of the design. This is done in the same fashion as the top half. Just follow the graph drawing of the earring being worked.

12. Another place to tie off is on one of the loops that join the beads together along an outer edge of a design (Figure 11A). The knot is pulled down in the same fashion as explained in #10, on the previous page. All of the *tie off* loops are marked on each pattern next to the *exit* arrows.

11A.
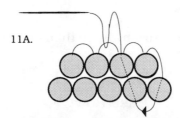

13. For those patterns that have an even number of beads in the BASE ROW, complete the first half of the design with both threads pointing up as shown below (Figures A and B).

A.   B.
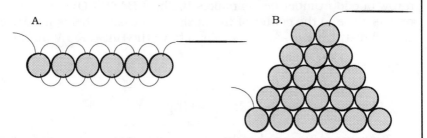

Attach needle to other section of thread, go through end bead on row above, around outside of that bead and through the end bead of the BASE ROW (Figure C below). Continue with rest of design.

C.
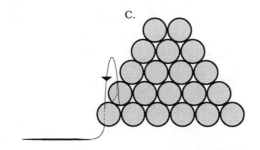

Increasing & Decreasing

To create sculptured designs there are just a few additional things to learn.

1. The BASE ROW is not always the widest row in the design.

2. How to INCREASE by adding on more beads than in the previous row.

3. How to DECREASE a row by more than one bead at a time.

Base Row

Any row in a design can be the BASE ROW once increasing and decreasing has been learned. Being forced to taper a design from its largest point to its smallest point is no longer necessary. Preferably a row of odd number beads makes the best BASE ROW. Choosing one as close to the center of the design as possible helps for better thread distribution. All the designs have the BASE ROW marked.

Increasing

1. To increase just one bead at the beginning of a row, pick up two beads with the needle instead of the usual one. Then bring the needle through the top loop that goes between the last two beads of the first row, back up through the second bead on the thread, and pull down. (Figure #12)

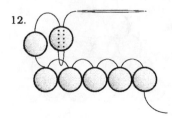

12.

2. To increase more than one bead at the beginning of a row, follow the preceding instructions for increasing just one bead. After the first two beads have been pulled down into place, go back through the first new bead on the row, add a bead, go through the same first bead and the bead below, up the next bead over and the bead where began. Going through the row below helps to reinforce. There are now three beads. (Figure #13) This can be extended out further if necessary. Continue with the rest of the row as instructed.

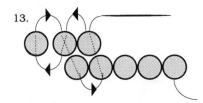

13.

3. To increase at the end of a row just completed, place a new bead on the thread, go down through the end bead of the previous row then back up through the new bead. (Figure #14)

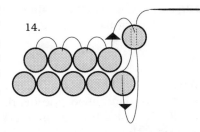

14.

4. To increase more than one bead at the end of a row, follow the above instructions for one bead. Pick up a new bead, go back through the last bead on the row and pull the two beads next to each other, then go back through the new bead. The row has now been extended by two and the needle is pointed down. Pick up another bead, go back through the last bead and pull the two beads together, then back up through the newest bead. The needle is now coming out the top and three extended beads have been added. (Figure #15) It is a lot like building a BASE ROW off the end of a row of beads.

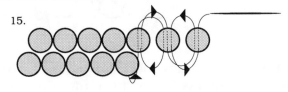

15.

5. Here is another way to extend just one bead at the end of a row. Pick up a new bead, pass the needle through the end thread of the previous row, pull the bead down, bring the needle back up through the new bead and pull down. (Figure # 16) This can only be done if there is an end thread. End threads are not on the end of every row.

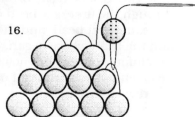
16.

Decreasing

Decreasing is just a matter of repositioning the needle by going through the bead work the shortest and easiest way. Planning out a route before starting is a good idea. It is very difficult to undo a mistake.

1. When a row of beads has been completed and the next row to be started is decreased one bead, drop down to the row of beads under the one just completed, and with the needle go down through the end bead, up through the bead next to it, and through the bead above and to the left. This brings the needle out of the bead one space over, ready to start a new row. (Figure #17)

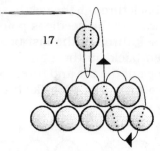
17.

2. To decrease two beads, just follow the above instructions but go down with the needle one more row, over one bead and up, coming out two beads over.

18.

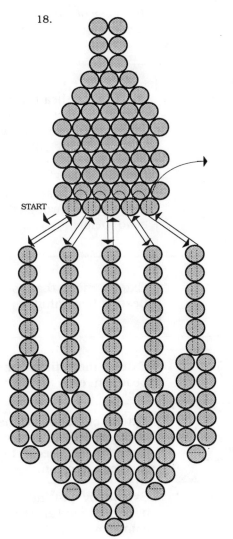

START

Horizontal fringe is very easy to make. (See Figure #18 to the left)

With the long section of thread left over after finishing the bottom section of the design, pick up the total amount of beads shown for the first fringe, go back through the first six beads forming a loop on the end. Run the needle up through the original bead along the bottom row of the design, and down the next bead over.

Repeat with the next fringe making sure to increase the length as shown. The fringe is usually tapered longer to the middle then shorter to other side, giving an arrow shape. Just follow the design being worked.

Symbols Used In Patterns

◆		Increase one bead at the beginning of new row.
▲		Increase one bead at end of row, connecting to the end thread of lower row.
✳		Increase one bead at end of row, going through the bead below.
●		Extend more than one bead at beginning.
◎		Extend more than one bead on end.
♥		Extend one bead. Done this way only to correct direction of needle for further extension.
■		Extend by putting one bead on thread and then going down through previous row repositioning to another part of the design.

Chapter
Two
Horizontal Patterns

The designs in this chapter are all sculptured with the BASE ROW running left to right (horizontal). A few are quite challenging. These are marked with five stars. The last three patterns in this chapter have fringe, which is explained on Page 19. Refer to Page 20 for the table of symbols used.

A number of patterns have an ear wire extension with a 4-bead loop, shown below. This helps the earring hang lower, clearing the ear wire, as in the Mallard earrings. Extensions are especially attractive on smaller earrings, dressing them up. They are usually added after the earring is complete and the balance point has been determined.

The example shown to the right is from the Mallard on Page 23. Follow the arrow down from START and up through DB bead marked. Add the beads for the extension, 4 beads for loop, and ear wire. Go down the extension and the DB bead, the bead below that and to the left, and up the bead to the right. Repeat this 2 to 3 times to reinforce, exit and tie off.

There may be slight variations to this. Follow the patterns closely.

White thread is primarily used throughout this book. This is because black thread shows through transparent or near transparent beads, changing their color. The Penguin on Page 22 has one side that is all dark. Using a black felt marking pen, darken the outer threads that are showing along the dark side. This can be done on any pattern. Apply carefully, as the black ink can wick up into a clear bead if the ink is applied too liberally.

Penguin

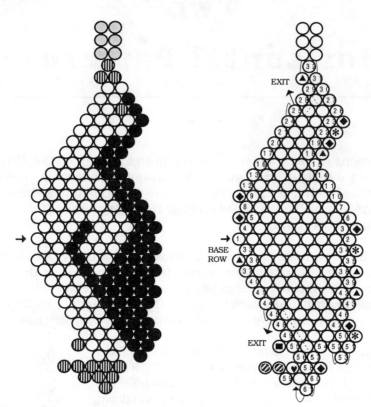

- ● Blue Iris
- ○ White Pearl
- ⊕ Semi-Matte S/L Squash
- ◉ Crystal (Clear)

BASE ROW 9 (DB) **
Thread - 1 1/2 yards, white. Place needle at 12 inches on thread.
Top Half
Follow #1- #32 . Add 6-bead loop with ear wire. Go down #32 and
▲, then up #31 and #32. Repeat to reinforce. Exit where shown.
Tie off on outer thread next to exit arrow, hide tail of thread and cut.
Bottom Half
Attach needle to second section of thread and begin with #33, follow
through to #58. Extend foot as shown. Continue with #59 - #61. Exit
where shown following dotted line. Tie off on outer thread next to exit
arrow, hide thread and cut.

Mallard

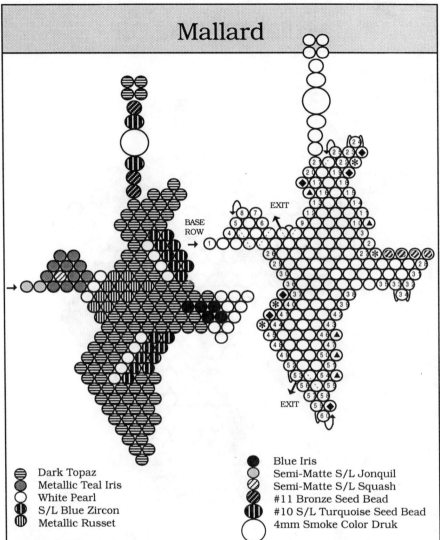

Legend:

- Dark Topaz
- Metallic Teal Iris
- White Pearl
- S/L Blue Zircon
- Metallic Russet
- Blue Iris
- Semi-Matte S/L Jonquil
- Semi-Matte S/L Squash
- #11 Bronze Seed Bead
- #10 S/L Turquoise Seed Bead
- 4mm Smoke Color Druk

BASE ROW 13 (DB) ***

Thread - 1 1/2 yards, white. Place needle at 12 inches on thread.

Top Half

Start with #1 - #6, turn. Complete duck's head, #7- #8. Reposition as shown, continue with #9 - #25. Reposition coming out #21. Attach beads for ear wire extension and 4-bead loop with ear wire. Go down extension, #21, #20, up bead to the right and #21. Repeat to reinforce. Exit where shown. Tie off on loop next to exit arrow, hide tail of thread and cut.

Bottom Half

Attach needle to the other section of thread, begin with #26 - #27. Extend as shown. Continue with #28 - #60. Exit where shown. Tie off on side loop next to exit arrow, hide thread and cut.

Mallard Taking Off

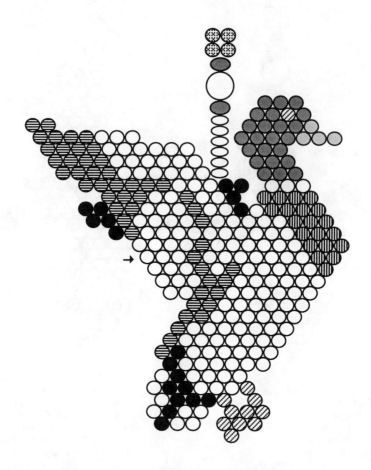

○ White Pearl		⊕ Crystal (Clear)
⊜ Dark Topaz Luster		◉ Semi-Matte S/L Jonquil
◍ Metallic Russet		◍ #11 Clear Green Seed Bead
◉ Metallic Teal Iris		◉ #12 Clear Seed Bead
● Blue Iris		◯ 4mm Smoke Color Druk
⊘ Semi-Matte S/L Squash		

BASE ROW 13 (DB) ****
Thread - 2 1/4, white. Place needle at 24 inches on thread.
Top Half
Begin with #1, follow through to #10, turn. Complete neck and head,
#11 - #28. Reposition as shown (dotted line) for #29 - #42. Reposition
coming out #32. At this point add beads for extension, 4-bead loop
and ear wire. Go down extension, bead to left of #32, and up #32.

Mallard Taking Off

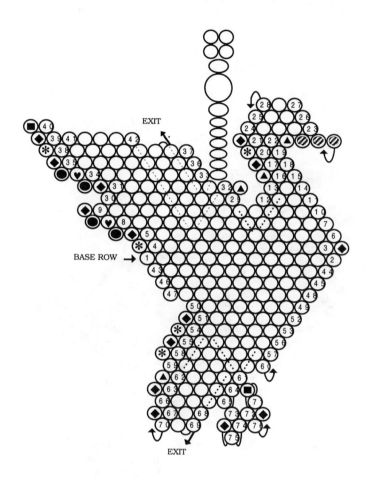

Repeat to reinforce. Follow dotted line to exit design. Tie off on outer loop next to exit arrow, hide tail of thread and cut.

Bottom Half
Attach needle to other section of thread and begin with #43 - #64 & ◉. Continue with #65 - #70. Reposition (see dotted line) coming out ◉ to the right of #64. Create an outer thread on ◉ . Attach #71 to that outer thread, turn. Attach ◉ and #72 to inner thread of #71. Add #73 connecting to side thread of #65. Loop back around through #72 and #73 to reinforce. Complete to #76. Go up through leg and down through tail exiting where shown. Tie off on loop next to exit arrow, hide thread and cut.

Wood Duck

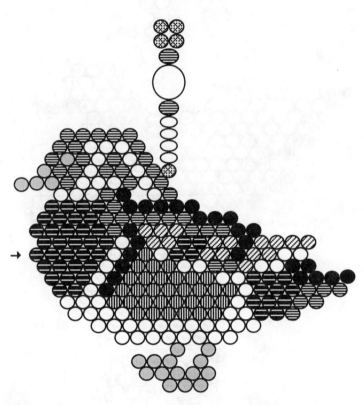

- Metallic Teal Iris
- White Pearl
- Blue Iris
- S/L Blue Zircon
- Lined Peach AB
- Metallic Russet

- Semi-Matte Squash
- Crystal (Clear)
- #12 Clear Seed Bead
- #11 Clear Green Seed Bead
- 4mm Smoke Color Druk

BASE ROW 18 (DB) ***

Thread - 2 yards, white. Place needle at 18 inches on thread.

Top Half

Start at #1 and follow through to #14. Extend for beak. Continue with #15 - #16. Add ⓐ to side thread of #13 and second ⓐ to side thread of #12. Loop around two ⓐ, then extend ⊘. Continue with #17 - #24. Reposition coming out top of ⊙. Attach beads for ear wire extension and 4-bead loop with ear wire. Go down extension beads, ⊙, ⊘, #12, up #11⊘ & ⊙. Repeat to reinforce. Exit head, tie off on loop next to exit arrow. Hide tail of thread and cut.

Wood Duck

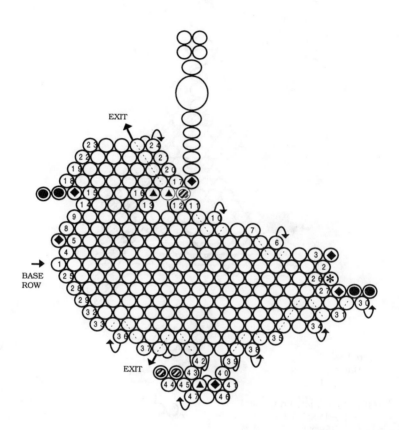

Bottom Half

Attach needle to other section of thread, begin with #25 - #26. Extend at beginning of row #27, then continue with rest of design to #38. Add #39 making sure there are two outer threads. Connect #40 to inner (left) thread, turn, add ● and #41. Go back through ●, leg, and over two beads. Add #42 making sure there are two outer threads. Connect #43 to outer (left) thread. Extend two beads. Continue with #44, #45 and ▲. Loop ▲ and ● together, then back through ● and out #41. Finish with #46 - #47. Go up through leg and body two rows, then out where shown. Tie off on loop next to exit arrow. Hide tail of thread and cut.

Rearing Horse

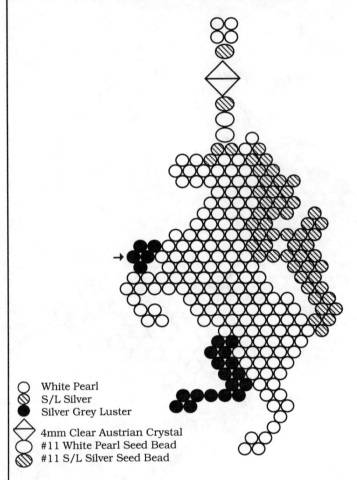

○ White Pearl
⊗ S/L Silver
● Silver Grey Luster
◇ 4mm Clear Austrian Crystal
○ #11 White Pearl Seed Bead
⊘ #11 S/L Silver Seed Bead

BASE ROW 11 (DB) ***** *Do not include tail beads in BASE ROW.*
Thread - 1 3/4 yards, white. Place needle at 14 inches on thread.
Top Half
Start at #1, continue to #4. Reposition to #5 (see dotted line),
continue through #16. Extend as shown, continue with #17 - #23.
Reposition (see dotted line), add beads for ear wire extension and 4
bead loop with ear wire. Go down extension and #21, then up bead
to right. Repeat to reinforce. Exit where shown. Tie off on loop next
to exit arrow, hide and cut thread.

Bottom Half
Attach needle to other section of thread, begin with #24 - #28. Extend
out connecting ⊕ 's to outer threads of #25 and #24, loop ⊕ and

Rearing Horse

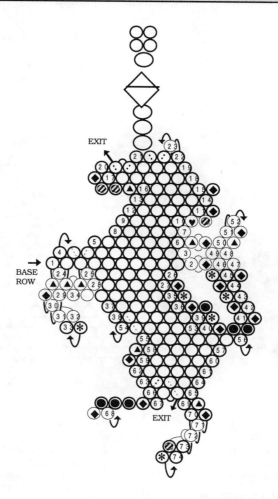

⊕ together where shown. Start front leg with ⊛ and #29, turn. Add #30 creating two outer threads. Connect #31 to right thread of #30. Extend with #32, looping back through #31. Add #33 and ⊛. Reposition coming out #29 and continue with #34 - #40. Extend for tail as shown. Follow #41 - #52 carefully, connecting tail to mane where shown. Reposition coming out #40. Continue with #53 - #66, turn. Add ⊛ and #67, extend for leg, turn. Add ⊛ and #68. Reposition for #69 - #70. Add #71 creating two outer threads. Connect #72 to left thread of #71. Create left outer thread for #72. Connect #73 to left thread of #72. Extend one bead. Coming out #73, add #74 and ⊛. Go back through #74, up leg and out between hind legs where shown. Tie off, hide tail of thread and cut.

Peregrine

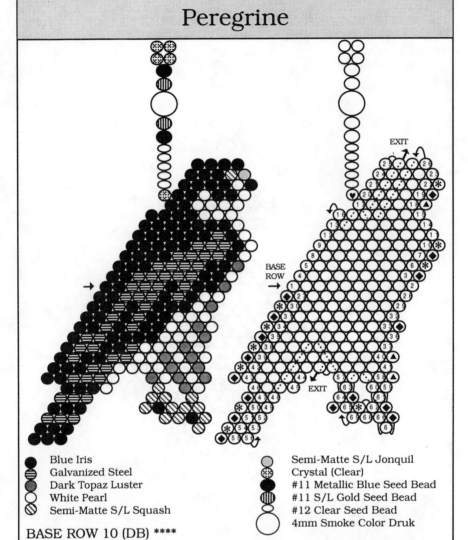

Blue Iris
Galvanized Steel
Dark Topaz Luster
White Pearl
Semi-Matte S/L Squash

Semi-Matte S/L Jonquil
Crystal (Clear)
#11 Metallic Blue Seed Bead
#11 S/L Gold Seed Bead
#12 Clear Seed Bead
4mm Smoke Color Druk

BASE ROW 10 (DB) ****

Thread 1 3/4 yards, white. Place needle 16 inches in on thread.

Top Half

Start with #1 - #20, add ⊕. Continue with #21 - #26. Reposition coming out ⊕. Attach beads for extension and 4-bead loop with ear wire. Go down extension, ⊕, #17, bead to left below, up bead to right, #17 and ⊕. Repeat to reinforce. Tie off where shown, cut.

Bottom Half

Attach needle to other section of thread, begin with #27 - #44. Complete tail, #45 - #56. Reposition, continue with #57 - #62. Go back through ⧓ and reposition for #63 - ⊛. Loop ⊛ to #62, back down #62 and out ⧓. Complete #66 - #69. Tie off on loop under tail. Hide thread and cut.

Grapes

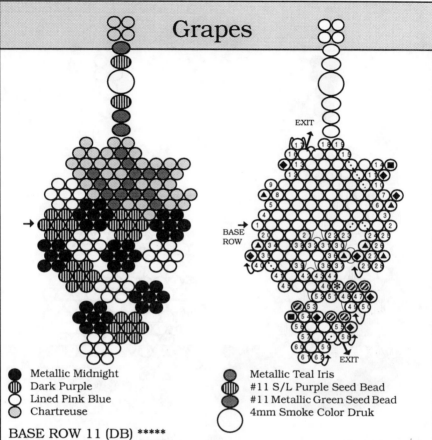

● Metallic Midnight
◍ Dark Purple
○ Lined Pink Blue
◉ Chartreuse

● Metallic Teal Iris
◍ #11 S/L Purple Seed Bead
◉ #11 Metallic Green Seed Bead
○ 4mm Smoke Color Druk

BASE ROW 11 (DB) *****

Thread - 1 1/2 yards, white. Place needle at 14 inches on thread.

Top Half

Start with #1- #19. Attach beads for ear wire extension and 4-bead loop with ear wire. Go down extension and #18, up #19. Repeat to reinforce. Tie off where shown, hide tail of thread and cut.

Bottom Half

Attach needle to other section of thread, begin with #20 - #25, turn. Complete #26 - #29. Reposition coming out #23. Add #30, connect #31 to side thread of #22, #32 to side thread of #21. Loop together to reinforce. Continue to #36 and ⦿. Loop ⦿ and ◉ together, turn. Continue with #37 - #41. Connect #42 to side thread of #39, #43 to side thread of #38. Loop together to reinforce. Add #44. Reposition coming out #41, continue with #45 - #46. Extend, turn, add #47 - #50. Reposition coming out #48. Attach #51 - #52. Create an outer thread on #52, turn. Attach #53 to #52 outer thread, extend one. Add ◉ , #54 . Extend with ◼. Coming out #54 extend two beads past ◉ . Go back through last extended bead, catch outer thread of #49 and come back through. Continue with #55 - #62. Tie off where shown and cut.

Junk

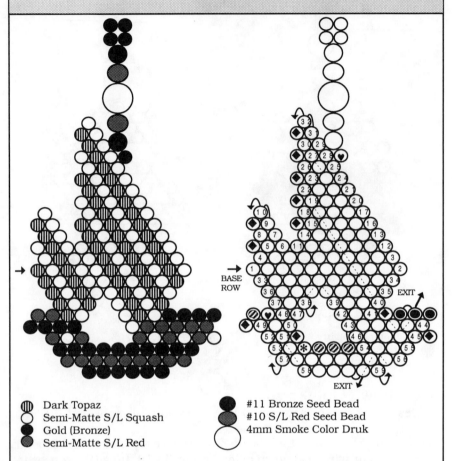

(Dark Topaz symbol) Dark Topaz	(#11 symbol) #11 Bronze Seed Bead
(Squash symbol) Semi-Matte S/L Squash	(#10 symbol) #10 S/L Red Seed Bead
(Gold symbol) Gold (Bronze)	(Druk symbol) 4mm Smoke Color Druk
(Red symbol) Semi-Matte S/L Red	

BASE ROW 11 (DB) ***
Thread, 1 1/4 yards, white. Place needle at 12 inches on thread.
Top Half
Begin with #1 - #6. Turn and complete small sail, #7 - #10. Reposition coming out #6. Continue with #11 - #32. Reposition (see dotted line) coming out ♥. Attach beads for ear wire extension and 4-bead loop with ear wire. Go down extension and #28, up ♥. Repeat to reinforce. Exit design where shown <u>after bottom half is complete</u>. Tie off on loop next to exit arrow. Hide thread and cut.
Bottom Half
Attach needle to other section of thread, begin with #33 - #40. Extend out at #41 and complete front part of boat through #46. Reposition (see dotted line) coming out #38. Continue with #47 - #53. Extend as shown, attach last extended bead to side loop of #46. Complete #54 - #59. Tie off on bottom loop, hide thread and cut.

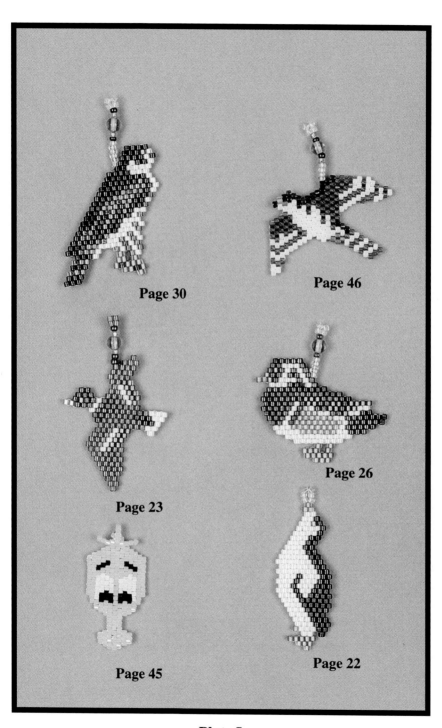

Page 30

Page 46

Page 23

Page 26

Page 45

Page 22

Plate I

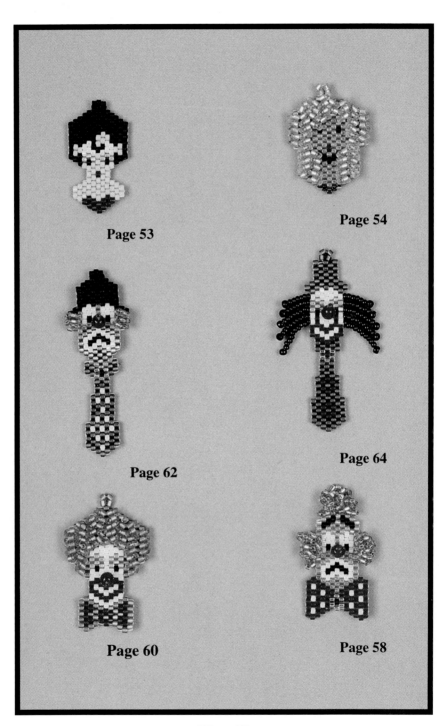

Page 53

Page 54

Page 62

Page 64

Page 60

Page 58

Plate II

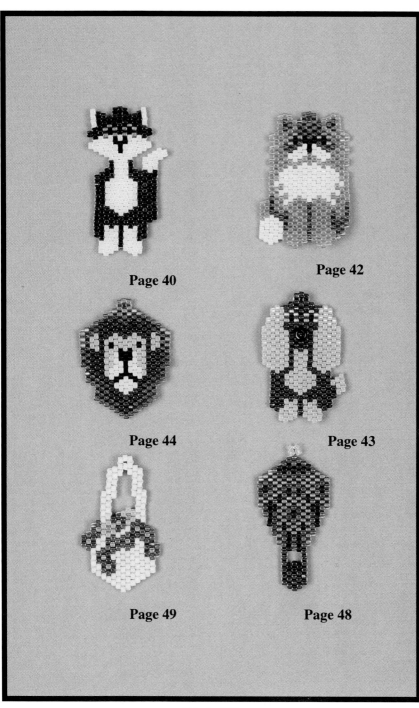

Page 40

Page 42

Page 44

Page 43

Page 49

Page 48

Plate III

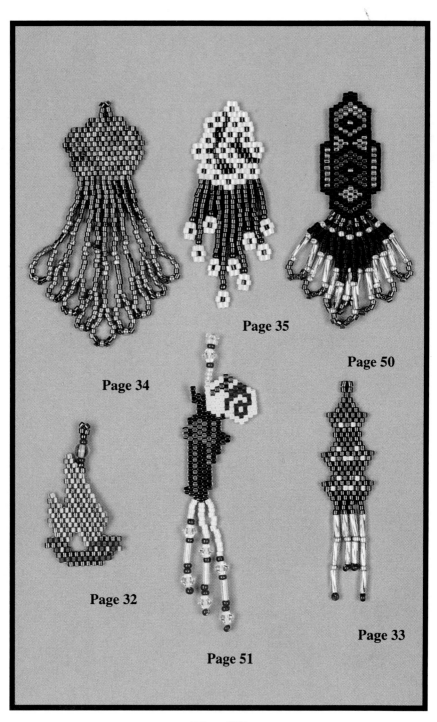

Page 34

Page 35

Page 50

Page 32

Page 51

Page 33

Plate IV

Pagoda

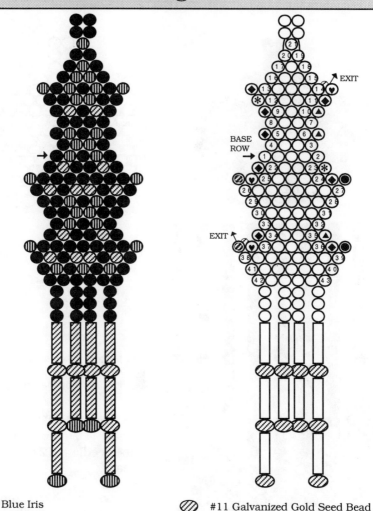

- ● Blue Iris
- ◫ S/L Red
- ⊘ Galvanized Gold
- ⊘ #11 Galvanized Gold Seed Bead
- ⬤ #11 S/L Red Seed Bead
- ▨ 2x6mm Gold Twist Bugle

BASE ROW 5 (DB) **
Thread - 1 1/2 yards, black. Place needle at 10 inches on thread.
Top Half
Start at #1 - #21. Add 4-bead extend loop with ear wire. Go down #21, #19, up #20 and #21. Repeat to reinforce. Tie off on loop next to exit arrow, hide thread and cut.
Bottom Half
Attach needle to other section of thread, begin with #22 - #43. Add fringe as shown centering two outer fringe between two lower beads of design. Tie off on loop where shown. Hide thread tail and cut.

Sculptured Rose

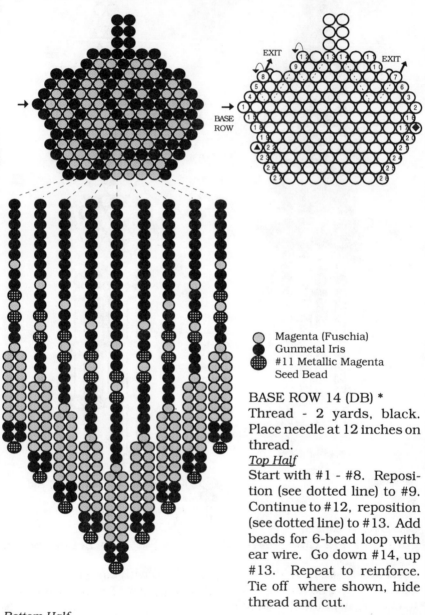

Magenta (Fuschia)
Gunmetal Iris
#11 Metallic Magenta
Seed Bead

BASE ROW 14 (DB) *
Thread - 2 yards, black.
Place needle at 12 inches on
thread.

Top Half
Start with #1 - #8. Reposition (see dotted line) to #9.
Continue to #12, reposition
(see dotted line) to #13. Add
beads for 6-bead loop with
ear wire. Go down #14, up
#13. Repeat to reinforce.
Tie off where shown, hide
thread and cut.

Bottom Half
Attach needle to other section of thread. Begin with #15 and
continue through to #28. Add fringe as shown above. Exit along top
of design, tie off on loop, hide thread and cut.

Bouquet

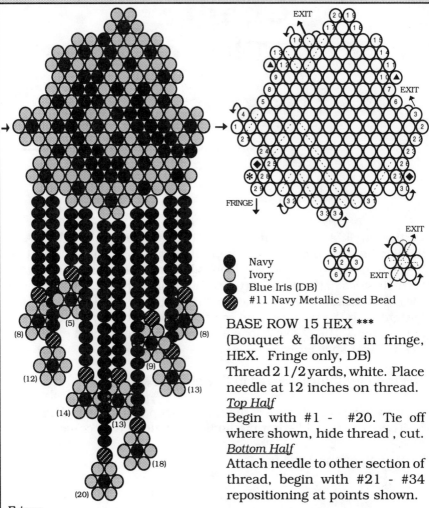

- ● Navy
- ○ Ivory
- ● Blue Iris (DB)
- ◉ #11 Navy Metallic Seed Bead

BASE ROW 15 HEX *
(Bouquet & flowers in fringe, HEX. Fringe only, DB)
Thread 2 1/2 yards, white. Place needle at 12 inches on thread.
Top Half
Begin with #1 - #20. Tie off where shown, hide thread, cut.
Bottom Half
Attach needle to other section of thread, begin with #21 - #34 repositioning at points shown.

Fringe
Create (10) individual (7-bead) flowers, shown above (see page 57 for written instructions). To attach, go down #5 bead of flower and up #4 bead. Attach fringe as shown. The amount of DB beads used for each fringe is shown in parenthesis next to flowers. Tie off on loop next to exit arrow and cut. If fringe does not hang straight, wet earring, arrange on a flat cloth surface, weigh down and let dry. A post with 10mm pad can be glued directly on back of earring using E-6000™ adhesive. Or cut a piece of black leather to fit shape of earring, create a hole for the earring post to come through and glue both post and leather to back of design. Make sure main part of earring is reverse image of the other before gluing. Let dry overnight.

Chapter
Three
Vertical Earrings

Vertical style earrings differ from other designs in that the BASE ROW runs from the bottom, where the fringe is usually connected, to the top, where the ear wire loop is located. The beads are sitting on their sides in the main part of the earring with thread coming out the sides. In a horizontal style earring the BASE ROW runs from left to right with the beads sitting so that the thread comes out the top and bottom. The ear wire loop and fringe are connected differently to a vertical style earring.

The two new things covered in this chapter are:

1. How to form and connect the ear wire loop to the Vertical Earring. There are two different methods: Extended & Recessed.

2. How to connect the fringe.

Extended Ear Wire Loop

The easiest way to form an ear wire loop on vertical style earrings is to create a loop at the end of the BASE ROW (optional for any pattern).

19.   Add an extra bead to the BASE ROW if the pattern shows it recessed. The extra bead will complete the tapered point of the design from which the loop will be extended. (Figure #19)

1. Reinforce the last bead by going back through the previous bead then back through the end bead. (Figure #20) Pick up 4 beads with the needle, run back through the last bead of the BASE ROW, and pull into place. (Figure #20)

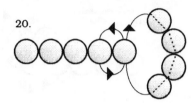

20.

2. Loop around 2 to 3 times to reinforce the ear wire loop. (Figure #21) Continue with the design.

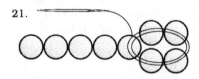

21.

Recessed Ear Wire Loop

The recessed ear wire loop is more difficult to make, but the end result looks more professional. The loop is more like a part of the earring than just an extension. (Figure #22)

22.

1. Complete the BASE ROW (reinforce the last two beads by looping around a second time). On the next row, increase one bead as shown, then run needle back through the first bead. (Figure #23)

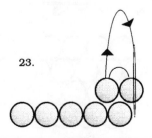

23.

2. Increase with a second bead (Figure #24), reposition to where started. Finish the row and first half of the design. Tie off, hide the tail of thread and cut.

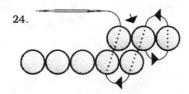

24.

3. Attach the needle to the second section of thread. Complete the row next to the BASE ROW, extending it out to match the row on the other side of the BASE ROW. (Figure #25) Pick up a bead, run the needle through the end bead of the other extended row and pull the bead into place. (Figure #25) Complete loop.

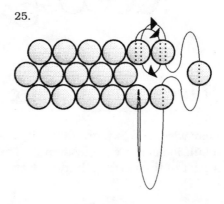

25.

4. Reinforce 2 to 3 times by going through the 6 beads that form the loop. (Figure #26) Complete the last half of the design. Tie off and cut the thread only if there is no fringe to the design.

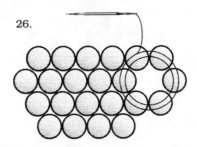

26.

Fringe For Vertical Earrings

The fringe off the bottom of a Vertical Earring is constructed differently because the beads in the main part of the design are turned sideways, causing the thread to come out the sides of the design instead of the bottom. (Figure #27)

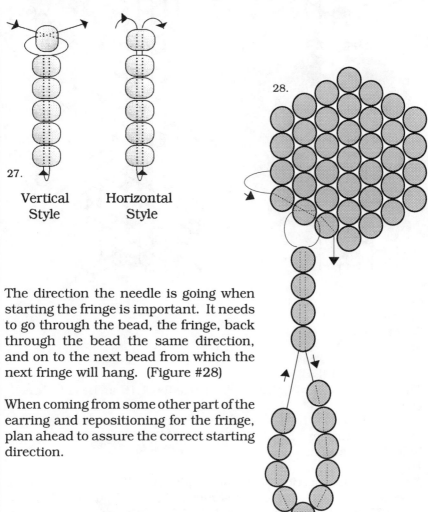

27.

Vertical
Style

Horizontal
Style

28.

The direction the needle is going when starting the fringe is important. It needs to go through the bead, the fringe, back through the bead the same direction, and on to the next bead from which the next fringe will hang. (Figure #28)

When coming from some other part of the earring and repositioning for the fringe, plan ahead to assure the correct starting direction.

Alley Cat

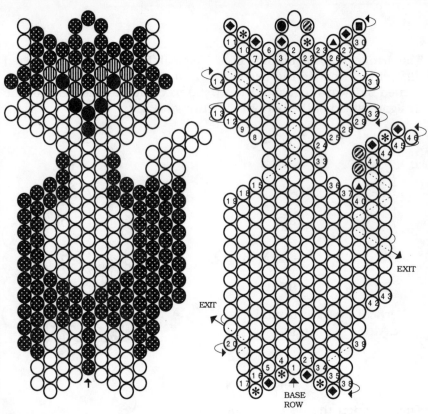

- ⬤ Blue Iris
- ◯ White Pearl
- ● Matte Black
- ◍ Semi-Matte S/L Squash

BASE ROW 21 (DB) **

Thread - 1 3/4 yards, white. Place needle at 16 inches on thread.

Left Half

Start with #1 - #8, turn. Complete left side of cat's head. Reposition (see dotted line) for #15 - #20. Tie off on outer loop next to exit arrow, hide thread and cut.

Right Half

Attach to other section of thread, begin with #21 - #22. Create a recessed style ear wire loop just after #22 (See Figures #23 - #26, Pages 37 & 38). Continue with #23 - #24, turn and complete right side of cat's head. Reposition after #32 coming out #24. Continue with #33 - #46. Zig-zag through tail to strengthen. Tie off on outer loop next to exit arrow, hide thread and cut.

Siamese Cat

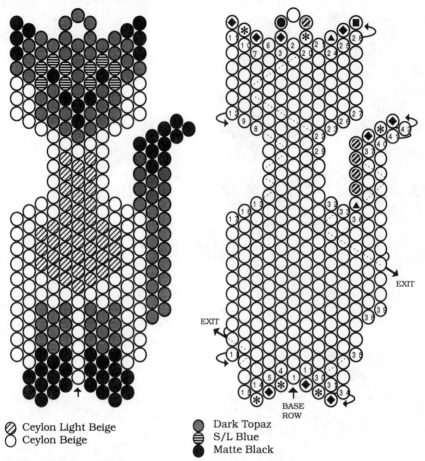

⊘ Ceylon Light Beige
○ Ceylon Beige

◓ Dark Topaz
⊜ S/L Blue
● Matte Black

BASE ROW 23 (DB) **
Thread - 2 yards, white. Place needle at 18 inches on thread.
Left Half
Begin with #1 - #8, turn. Complete left side of cat's head, #9 - #12.
Reposition (see dotted line) for #13 - #18. Tie off on outer loop, hide
thread and cut.
Right Half
Attach to other section of thread, begin with #19 - #20. Create
recessed style ear wire loop just after #20 (See Figures #23 - #26,
Pages 37 & 38). Continue with #21 - #22, turn and complete right
side of cat's head. Reposition after #28 (dotted line) coming out #22.
Continue with #29 - #36. Extend tail two beads longer than Alley
Cat's tail. Continue to #42. Zig-zag through tail to strengthen. Tie
off on outer loop next to exit arrow.

Persian Cat

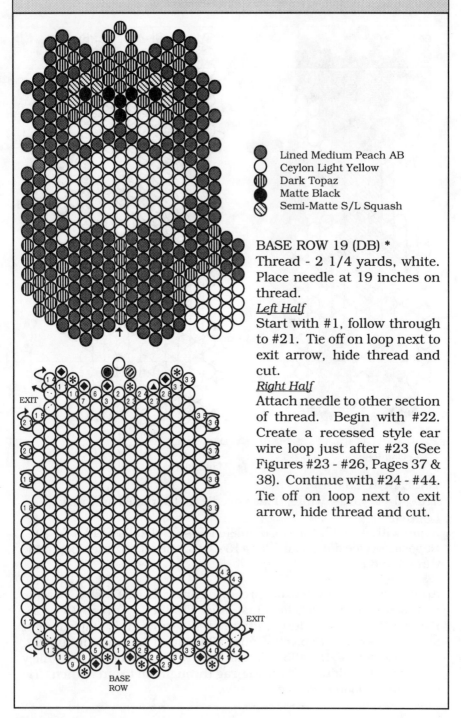

Lined Medium Peach AB
Ceylon Light Yellow
Dark Topaz
Matte Black
Semi-Matte S/L Squash

BASE ROW 19 (DB) *
Thread - 2 1/4 yards, white.
Place needle at 19 inches on
thread.
Left Half
Start with #1, follow through
to #21. Tie off on loop next to
exit arrow, hide thread and
cut.
Right Half
Attach needle to other section
of thread. Begin with #22.
Create a recessed style ear
wire loop just after #23 (See
Figures #23 - #26, Pages 37 &
38). Continue with #24 - #44.
Tie off on loop next to exit
arrow, hide thread and cut.

Big Eared Dog

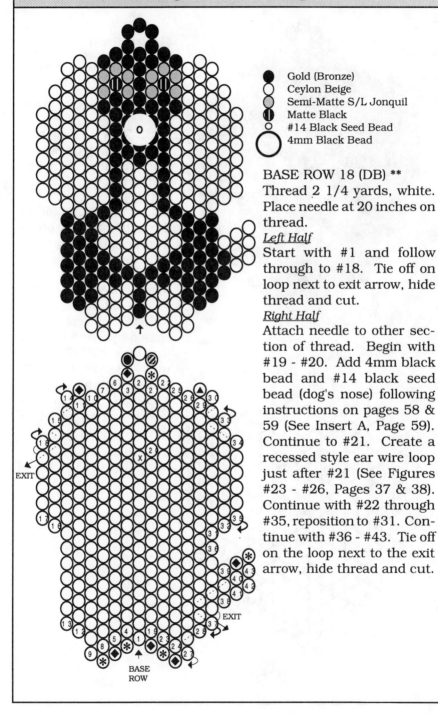

● Gold (Bronze)
○ Ceylon Beige
◐ Semi-Matte S/L Jonquil
◐ Matte Black
○ #14 Black Seed Bead
◯ 4mm Black Bead

BASE ROW 18 (DB) **
Thread 2 1/4 yards, white. Place needle at 20 inches on thread.

Left Half
Start with #1 and follow through to #18. Tie off on loop next to exit arrow, hide thread and cut.

Right Half
Attach needle to other section of thread. Begin with #19 - #20. Add 4mm black bead and #14 black seed bead (dog's nose) following instructions on pages 58 & 59 (See Insert A, Page 59). Continue to #21. Create a recessed style ear wire loop just after #21 (See Figures #23 - #26, Pages 37 & 38). Continue with #22 through #35, reposition to #31. Continue with #36 - #43. Tie off on the loop next to the exit arrow, hide thread and cut.

Lion

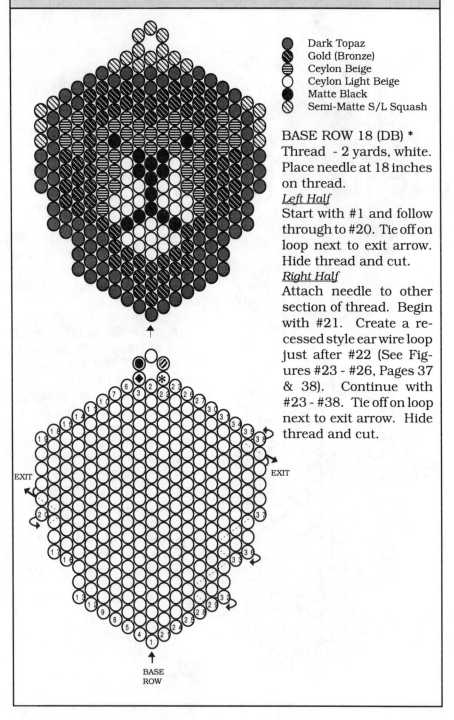

- ⬤ Dark Topaz
- ⬤ Gold (Bronze)
- ⬤ Ceylon Beige
- ⬤ Ceylon Light Beige
- ⬤ Matte Black
- ⬤ Semi-Matte S/L Squash

BASE ROW 18 (DB) *
Thread - 2 yards, white.
Place needle at 18 inches
on thread.
Left Half
Start with #1 and follow
through to #20. Tie off on
loop next to exit arrow.
Hide thread and cut.
Right Half
Attach needle to other
section of thread. Begin
with #21. Create a re-
cessed style ear wire loop
just after #22 (See Fig-
ures #23 - #26, Pages 37
& 38). Continue with
#23 - #38. Tie off on loop
next to exit arrow. Hide
thread and cut.

EXIT

EXIT

BASE
ROW

Yellow Ducky

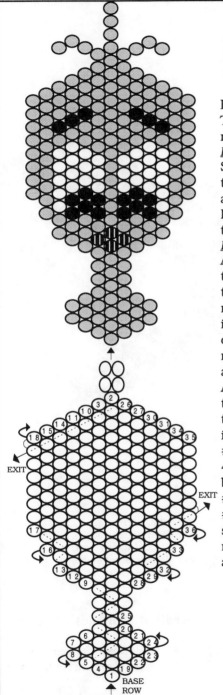

○ Yellow
● Black
○ White Pearl
◐ Yellow/Orange

BASE ROW 22 (HEX) **
Thread - 2 yards, white. Place needle at 18 inches on thread.
Left Half
Start with #1. Add a 4-bead extended ear wire loop with ear wire after #2 (See Figures #20 & #21, Page 37). Continue with #3 through #18. Do Not Tie Off.
Right Half
Attach needle to other section of thread, begin with #19 - #20, turn. Complete section below neck, #21 - #24. Reposition coming out #20. Complete rest of design, #25 - #36. Tie off on loop next to exit arrow, hide thread and cut.

Attach needle to first section of thread, reposition going back through head coming out #2 (see insert below). Extend 4 beads, #37 - #38. Work back to #2. Add 4 beads to thread, #39 - #40, go back through three of them and #2. Repeat on other side of #2, #41 - #42. Exit design where shown on left side. Tie off on loop next to exit arrow. Hide thread and cut.

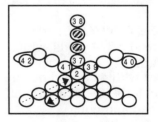

Flying Peregrine

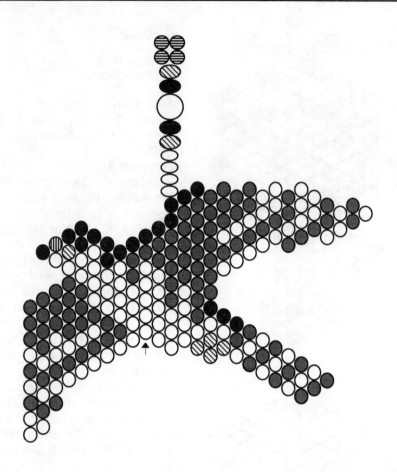

● Blue Iris		⊜ Crystal (Clear)	
◉ Dark Topaz		⊗ #12 Clear Seed Bead	
○ White Pearl		⊘ #11 S/L Gold Seed Bead	
⊗ Semi-Matte S/L Squash		● #11 Metallic Blue Seed Bead	
⦀ Semi-Matte S/Lined Jonquil		○ 4mm Smoke Color Druk	

BASE ROW 7 (DB) ***
Thread 1 3/4 yards, white. Position needle at 15 inches on thread.
Left Half
Start with #1 and continue through to #17. Reposition (see dotted line) for #18 - #23. Tie off where shown next to exit arrow. Hide thread and cut.

Flying Peregrine

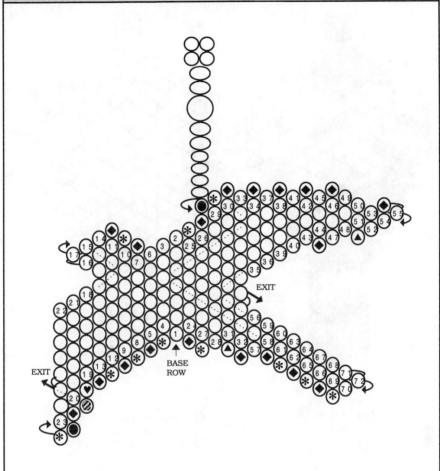

Right Half

Attach needle to other section of thread, start with #24 - #35. Turn and complete wing, #36 - #55. Reposition (see dotted line) and continue with #56 - #72. Reposition following dotted line coming out ✱ on front of right wing for the ear wire extension. Add beads for extension and 4-bead loop with ear wire. Go down extension, through ◉, #29 and ✱. Repeat to reinforce. Go through body (no dotted lines shown) and exit under right wing where shown with exit arrow. Tie off on loop, hide thread and cut.

Hot Air Balloon

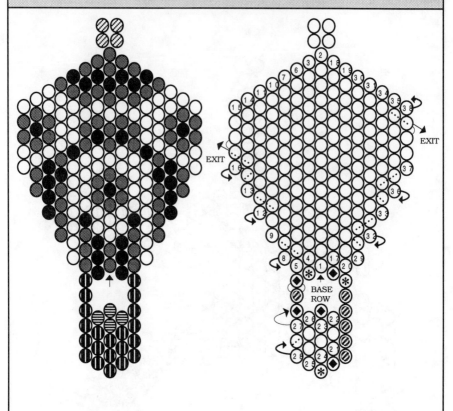

○ Semi-Matte S/L Purple	🌑 Gold (Bronze)
◉ Magenta (Fuschia)	⊜ Blue Iris
● S/L Violet	⊘ Crystal (Clear)

BASE ROW 15 (DB) **
Thread - 1 3/4 yards, white. Place needle at 16 inches on thread.
Left Half
Begin with #1 - #2. Add 4-bead extended ear wire loop with ear wire after #2 (See Figures #20 & #21, Pages 37). Continue with #3 - #4. Extend just the ◉ at #5. Basket will be created later. Continue with #6 - #16. Tie off on loop next to exit arrow. Hide thread and cut.
Right Half
Attach needle to other section of thread, begin with #17 - #20. Extend as shown. Continue with #21 - #28. Reposition to beginning of row, needle pointing right. Extend one bead, loop ⊘ and ◉ together. Reposition coming out #20. Continue with rest of design, #29 - #38. Exit where shown, tie off on loop next to exit arrow. Hide thread and cut.

Flower Basket

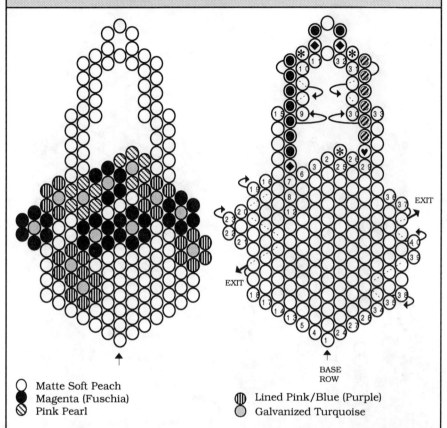

○ Matte Soft Peach
● Magenta (Fuschia)
◍ Pink Pearl

◍ Lined Pink/Blue (Purple)
◌ Galvanized Turquoise

BASE ROW
EXIT
EXIT

BASE ROW 13 (DB) *****
Thread - 1 3/4 yards, white. Place needle 16 inches on thread.
Left Half
Start with #1 - #8. Extend above ◉ as shown. Zig-zag back through extended beads coming out fifth bead down. Continue with #9 - #11. Reinforce ◉ & ◉ . Follow arrow back through coming out #8. Continue with #12 - #15. Reposition coming out fifth bead down, and finish with #16 - #23. Exit where shown. Tie off and cut.
Right Half
Attach needle to the other section of thread, begin with #24 - #29. Extend as shown. Zig-zag back through extension coming out fifth bead down. Continue with #30 - #32. Extend one bead past ◉ , reinforce. Insert bead between ◉ & ◉ at top of handle. Insert bead on bottom section between ◉ & ◉ . Loop around the six beads that make up the ear wire loop again to reinforce. Reposition coming out fourth bead down, continue with #33 - #40. Exit where shown. Tie off, hide thread and cut.

Mask

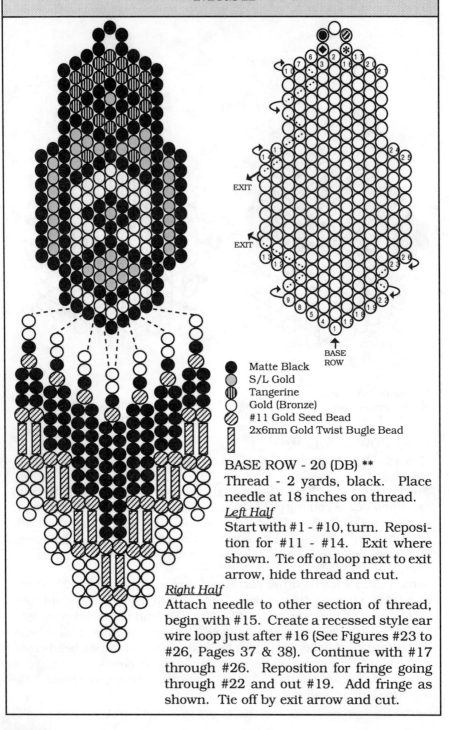

Matte Black
S/L Gold
Tangerine
Gold (Bronze)
#11 Gold Seed Bead
2x6mm Gold Twist Bugle Bead

BASE ROW - 20 (DB) **
Thread - 2 yards, black. Place needle at 18 inches on thread.

Left Half
Start with #1 - #10, turn. Reposition for #11 - #14. Exit where shown. Tie off on loop next to exit arrow, hide thread and cut.

Right Half
Attach needle to other section of thread, begin with #15. Create a recessed style ear wire loop just after #16 (See Figures #23 to #26, Pages 37 & 38). Continue with #17 through #26. Reposition for fringe going through #22 and out #19. Add fringe as shown. Tie off by exit arrow and cut.

Derringer

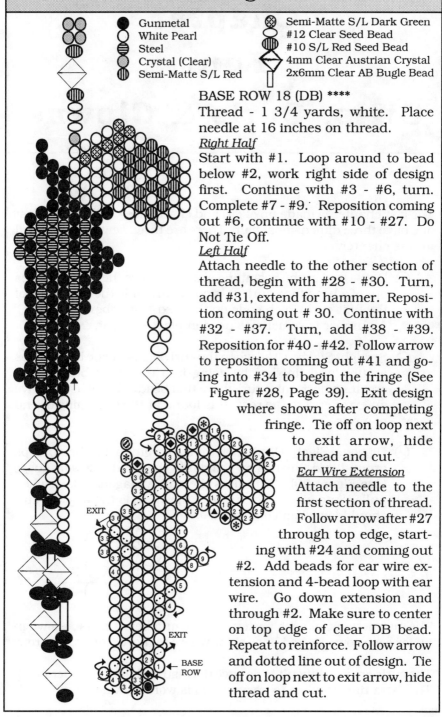

Legend:
- ● Gunmetal
- ○ White Pearl
- ⊜ Steel
- ◉ Crystal (Clear)
- ⊍ Semi-Matte S/L Red
- ⊗ Semi-Matte S/L Dark Green
- ⬭ #12 Clear Seed Bead
- ⊍ #10 S/L Red Seed Bead
- ◇ 4mm Clear Austrian Crystal
- ▯ 2x6mm Clear AB Bugle Bead

BASE ROW 18 (DB) ****

Thread - 1 3/4 yards, white. Place needle at 16 inches on thread.

Right Half

Start with #1. Loop around to bead below #2, work right side of design first. Continue with #3 - #6, turn. Complete #7 - #9. Reposition coming out #6, continue with #10 - #27. Do Not Tie Off.

Left Half

Attach needle to the other section of thread, begin with #28 - #30. Turn, add #31, extend for hammer. Reposition coming out # 30. Continue with #32 - #37. Turn, add #38 - #39. Reposition for #40 - #42. Follow arrow to reposition coming out #41 and going into #34 to begin the fringe (See Figure #28, Page 39). Exit design where shown after completing fringe. Tie off on loop next to exit arrow, hide thread and cut.

Ear Wire Extension

Attach needle to the first section of thread. Follow arrow after #27 through top edge, starting with #24 and coming out #2. Add beads for ear wire extension and 4-bead loop with ear wire. Go down extension and through #2. Make sure to center on top edge of clear DB bead. Repeat to reinforce. Follow arrow and dotted line out of design. Tie off on loop next to exit arrow, hide thread and cut.

Chapter
Four
Girls, Curls & Clowns

The last chapter is made up of girl and clown faces. All but the first one have three dimensional hair. There are three new symbols used in this chapter:

⊙ Dot: Used at the beginning of a row where the thread comes out of a bead for a curl. It is not a curl, only the beginning of the first curl which ends on the next bead above or below. A number is sometimes used in place of a dot.

⊖ Straight Slash: Used when the curl begins at one bead, loops around and finishes by going into the same bead. This creates a horizontal curl above that bead. This is used to give an extra curl to the row. It is found at the beginning or end of a row.

⊘ Diagonal Slash: Used when the curl begins at one bead, loops around and finishes by going into the bead below or above (See Figure 29). This gives the curl a diagonal slant when pulled into place. The angle of the slash is the way the curl should lay when completed.

29.

The instructions for each pattern list the number of curls , shown in ( ), for each row. Dotted lines show where to move from row to row.

The curls are not difficult to do once the instructions are understood. The extra time it takes to create them is worth taking.

Flapper Girl

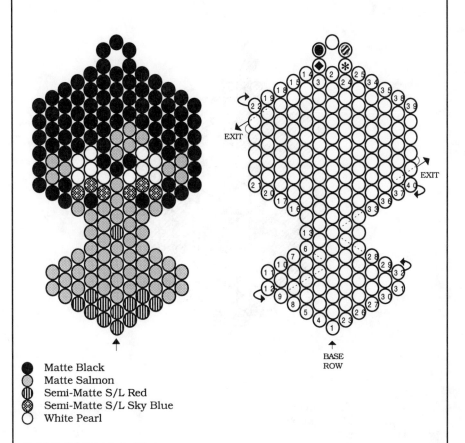

- ● Matte Black
- ○ Matte Salmon
- ◍ Semi-Matte S/L Red
- ▨ Semi-Matte S/L Sky Blue
- ○ White Pearl

BASE ROW 17 (DB) *
Thread - 1 1/2 yards, white. Position needle at 14 inches on thread.
Left Half
Start with #1 - #6, turn. Complete left shoulder, #7 - #12. Reposition, following arrow and dotted line, coming out #6. Continue with #13 - #22. Tie off on loop next to exit arrow, hide thread and cut.
Right Half
Attach needle to other section of thread, begin with #23. Create a recessed style ear wire loop just after #24 (See Figures #23 - #26, Pages 37 & 38). Continue with #25 - #28, turn. Complete right shoulder, #29 - #32. Reposition (see dotted line), continue with #33 through #40. Tie off on loop next to the exit arrow, hide thread and cut.

Blonde Curly Haired Girl

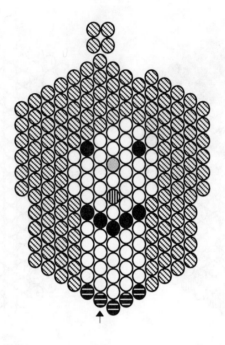

 Semi-Matte S/L Jonquil
Transparent Pink Luster
Matte Black
Semi-Matte S/L Red
Semi Matte S/L Medium Rose
Metallic Teal Iris

BASE ROW 16 (DB) ***
Thread - 2 1/4 yards, white. Position needle at 18 inches on thread.
Left Half
Start with #1. Add a 4-bead extended ear wire loop with ear wire after
#2 (See Figures #19 & #20, Pages 36 & 37). Continue with #3 - #14.
Exit design where shown and tie off on loop next to exit arrow. Hide
thread and cut.
Right Half
Attach needle to other section of thread, begin with #15. Complete
through #30. Do Not Tie Off.

Blonde Curly Haired Girl

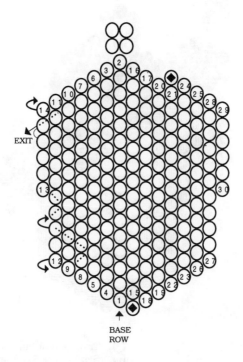

BASE
ROW

Curly Hair

Begin making curls using semi-matte silver-lined jonquil beads starting at #30 and using two beads per curl. (See Page 52) Repeat curls to end of row (5). Reposition by going through #28 and out #25 (needle pointing to left). Create curls down row #25 (11). Reposition to #22. Create curls up to face (5). Reposition, following dotted line, coming out bead with dot for bangs (3). Reposition to #17 and continue rest of curls, following diagram on right. Exit design where shown and tie off on loop next to exit arrow. Hide thread and cut.

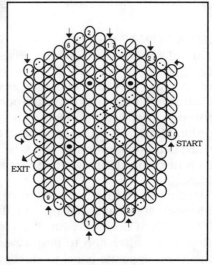

Girl With Hat

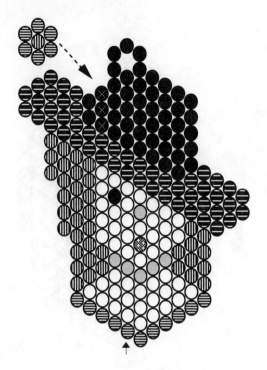

⊜ Gunmetal		○	Transparent Pink Luster
● Matte Black		◉	Semi-Matte S/L Dark Rose
⦷ Semi-Matte S/L Squash		⊜	Semi-Matte S/L Purple
		⊗	Semi-Matte S/L Red

BASE ROW 17 (DB) ****
Thread - 2 1/4 yards, white. Place needle at 18 inches on thread.
Left Half
Start with #1 - #12. Reposition as shown. Continue with #13 - #18.
Go through #15, out #6, needle pointing right. Add flower by looping
through first bead on center row of flower, back through #6 and
pulling flower down, second bead on flower then X-bead on design,
third bead on flower and last x-bead. Exit where shown. Tie off on
loop next to exit arrow, hide thread and cut.
Right Half
Attach needle to other section of thread, begin with #19. Create
recessed style ear wire loop just after #20 (Figures #23 - #26, Pages
37 & 38). Continue with #21 - #36, repositioning where shown.
Reposition after #36 to first straight slash on right of design (see
insert on opposite page) to start curls for hair.

Girl With Hat

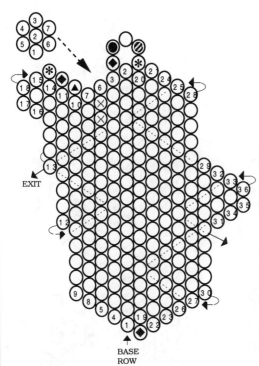

EXIT

BASE
ROW

Flower
BASE ROW 3 (DB)
Thread 12 inches, white.
Position needle 4 inches in
on thread.
Left Half
Begin with #1 - #5. Follow
arrow and dotted line to
exit (see diagram below).
Tie off on loop next to exit
arrow, hide tail of thread
and cut.
Right Half
Attach needle to the other
section of thread. Add #6
and #7. Exit as shown
below. Tie off, hide tail of
thread and cut.

EXIT

EXIT

Curly Hair
Follow diagram on right using
two semi-matte silver-lined
squash beads per curl. Start
with straight slash just below
hat on right, create a curl for
each slash (4) to end of row.
(See Page 52) Move to dot just
above shoulder on the next row,
go up to hat (3). Reposition to
dot on other side of face (see
dotted line) and go down (3), up
(9), down (6). Reposition and go
up (3). Exit the design where
shown. Tie off on loop next to
exit arrow, hide thread and cut.

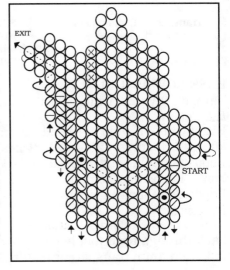

EXIT

START

Clown With Red Bow

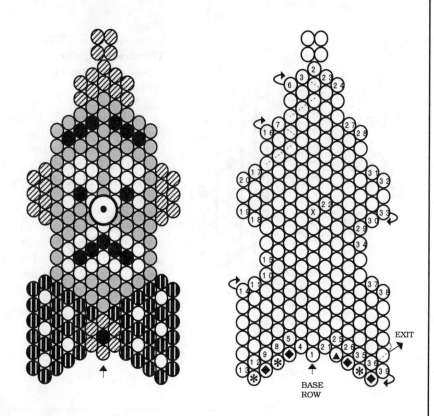

⊘ Transparent Pink Luster	⊘ S/L Gold
◯ White Pearl	◯ #14 Red Seed Bead
● Matte Black	◯ 4mm Transparent Red Druk
◖ Semi-Matte S/L Red	S/L Dark Gold HEX (Not Shown)

BASE ROW 19 (DB) ***

Thread - 2 yards, white. Position needle at 20 inches on thread.

Left Half

Begin with #1. Add a 4-bead extended ear wire loop with ear wire after #2 (Figures #20 - #21, Pages 37). Continue with #3 - #6. Reposition following arrow for #7 - #10, turn. Complete left side of bow. Reposition coming out #10 and continue with #15 - #16. Reposition following arrow for #17 - #20. Do Not Tie Off.

Right Half

Attach needle to other section of thread, begin with #21 - #22. Go back through bead just before #22 and X-bead (See Insert A, Page 59). Add 4mm transparent red druk bead and #14 red seed bead.

Clown With Red Bow

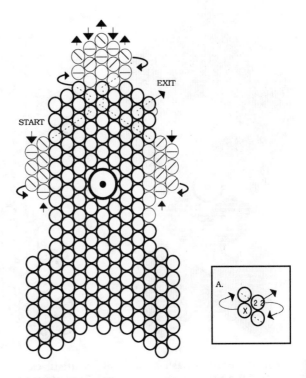

Go through druk bead and X-bead, pull down. Go through bead above X-bead and out #22. Continue with #23 - #29, turn. Complete right side of head, #30 - #33, reposition coming out #29. Complete rest of design #34 - #39. Exit design where shown and tie off on loop next to exit arrow. Hide thread and cut.

Curly Hair

Attach needle to first section of thread coming out #20 (START). Create first curl using five silver-lined dark gold HEX beads. Loop back through #20 bead, going right to left, to create first loop. (See Page 52) Add five HEX beads to thread, but this time go through the bead below. Continue, complete first row (3). Follow arrow to next row, going up creating (4) curls. Reposition following dotted line and arrow. Follow diagram above for hair on top of head. Reposition coming out *outer* row of hair on right side. Go down (3), up (4). Exit following dotted line. Tie off on loop next to exit arrow. Hide thread and cut.

Orange Curly Haired Clown

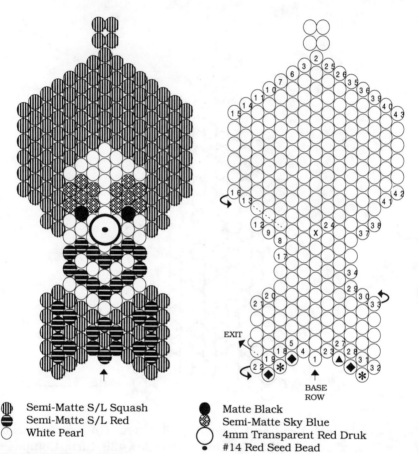

▥ Semi-Matte S/L Squash	⬤ Matte Black
⬤ Semi-Matte S/L Red	▦ Semi-Matte Sky Blue
◯ White Pearl	◯ 4mm Transparent Red Druk
	• #14 Red Seed Bead

BASE ROW 20 (DB) ***

Thread - 2 yards, white. Place needle at 18 inches on thread.

Left Half

Start with #1. Add 4-bead extended ear wire loop with ear wire after #2 (Figures #20 & #21, Page 37). Continue with #3 - #8, turn. Complete left side of head, #9 - #16. Reposition coming out #8. Continue with #17 - #22. Exit where shown. Tie off on loop next to exit arrow, hide thread and cut.

Right Half

Attach needle to other section of thread, begin with #23 - #24. Attach nose as explained on pages 58 and 59, Clown With Red Bow (See Figure A, Page 59). Continue with #24 - #29, turn. Complete right side of bow, #30 - #33. Reposition coming out #29. Complete rest of design, #34 - #43. Do Not Tie Off.

Orange Curly Haired Clown

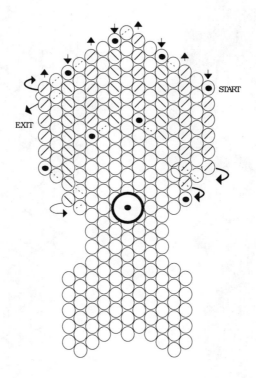

START

EXIT

Curly Half

Attach needle to first section of thread coming out #43 (START). Create loops (See Page 52) using two semi-matte silver-lined squash beads each. Loop through bead below first bead with dot on upper right corner of head (needle pointing right). Continue to end of row, down (5). Reposition two rows over (see arrow and dotted line). The needle is now pointing left, go up (8). Continue with down (5), up (5), down (5), up (5), and down (8). Reposition following arrow and dotted line coming out last row, lower left hand dot, needle is still pointing left. Go up last row (5). Exit design where shown. Tie off on loop next to exit arrow, hide thread and cut.

Hobo Clown

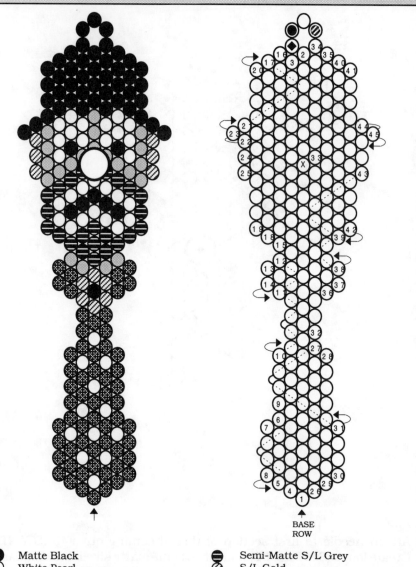

●	Matte Black	
○	White Pearl	
	Transparent Pink Luster	
	Semi-Matte S/L Medium Blue	
	Semi-Matte S/L Grey	
	S/L Gold	
○	4mm Transparent Red Druk	
●	#14 Red Seed Bead	
	S/L Dark Gold HEX (Not Shown)	

BASE ROW 29 (DB) ***

Thread - 2 yards, white. Position needle 20 inches in on thread.

Left Half

Begin with #1 - #6, turn. Complete bottom left corner of tie, #7 - #8.
Reposition coming out #6. Continue with #9 - #10. Reposition,

Hobo Clown

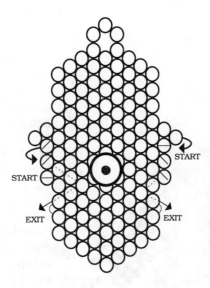

continue with #11 - #12, turn. Complete left side of necktie, #13 through #14. Reposition coming out #12. Continue with #15 - #20. Reposition, complete rest of left side, #21 - #25. Do Not Tie Off.

Right Half

Attach needle to other section of thread, begin with #26 - #27, turn. Complete right side of tie, #28 - #31. Reposition coming out #27. Continue with #32 - #33. Add druk bead and seed bead for nose (See Pages 58 - 59 and Figure A). Continue to #34. Create recessed style ear wire loop just after #34 (Figures #22 - #25, Pages 37 & 38). Continue with #35 through #38. Reposition, continue with #39 - #42. Reposition for #43 - #45. Do Not Tie Off.

Curly Hair

Follow diagram above. (See Page 52) Coming out #45 (START), complete curls using five silver-lined dark gold HEX beads each on the right side of head (3). Exit design where shown. Tie off on loop next to exit arrow, hide thread and cut.

Attach needle to first section of thread coming out #25 (START). Complete curls as shown for left side of head (3). Exit design where shown. Tie off on loop next to exit arrow, hide thread and cut.

Wild Hair Clown

❈	Semi-Matte S/L Medium Blue
⊜	Semi-Matte S/L Red
○	White Pearl
▓	Semi-Matte S/L Sky Blue
●	Matte Black

⊘	S/L Gold
●	#14 Black Seed Bead
●	#11 Black Seed Bead
○	4mm Transparent Red Druk
○	#14 Red Seed Bead

BASE ROW 28 (DB) ***
Thread - 2 yards, white. Position needle at 18 inches on thread.

Left Half

Begin with #1. Add 4 bead extended ear wire loop with ear wire after #2 (See Figures #20 & #21, Page 37). Continue with #3 - #6, turn. Complete left corner of tie, #7 through #8. Reposition coming out #6, complete #9 - #10. Reposition, continue with #11 through #12. Reposition (note heart symbol) following arrow and dotted line. Continue with #13 - #14 turn, add #15, continue to #16. Do Not Tie Off.

Right Half

Attach needle to the other section of thread, begin with #17 - #18, turn. Complete the right half of tie, #19 - #22. Reposition coming out #18. Continue with #23 - #24. Add druk and seed bead for nose (See Pages 58 - 59, and Figure A). Continue with #25 through #27, then #28 through #30. Do Not Tie Off.

Wild Hair Clown

Wild Hair

Coming out #30, follow the arrow through bead below and out bead below that. Add (6) #14 and (1) #11 black seed beads to thread. Go back through #14 seed beads, through DB bead in design and out DB bead below. Repeat following design below increasing with each row of #14 seed beads. Exit where shown. Tie off on loop next to exit arrow. Hide thread and cut.

Attach needle to thread coming out #16. Reposition following arrow and dotted line. Add (10) #14 and (1) #11 black seed beads to thread, go back through the (10) #14 beads, through DB bead in the design and out DB bead above. Decrease with each row of #14 seed beads as shown below. Exit design and tie off on loop next to exit arrow, hide thread and cut.

Wet earring, lay on a flat cloth surface, arrange hair to curve downward, weigh down and let dry.

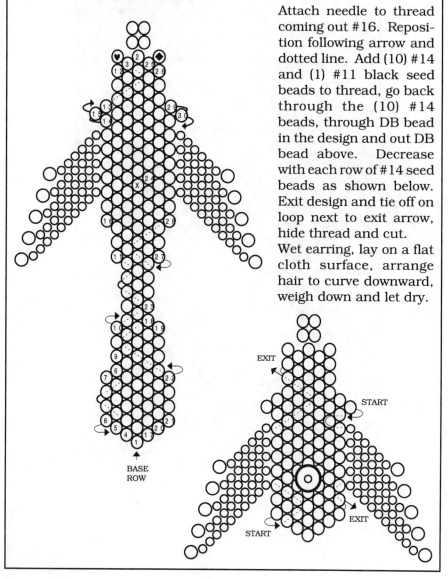

Horizontal DB Graph Paper

Vertical DB Graph Paper

Horizontal HEX Graph Paper

About
The Author

Barbara was born in San Francisco where she met and married her husband. Her creative talents surfaced early in their shared interest for oil painting. Later they moved, with their two sons, to the mountains in Northern California where she spent 12 years with the state park system. They currently reside in Redding, California.

Designing earrings came about only by accident. After purchasing a pair of beaded earrings for herself, Barbara became very curious as to how they were put together. This was only the beginning. Tiring of the basic patterns available, she soon began designing her own. Things moved quickly after that from sales to stores and involvement in art fairs, to her first book: *Beaded Images.*

SOME EAGLE'S VIEW PUBLISHING
BEST SELLERS THAT MAY BE OF INTEREST:

The Technique of Porcupine Quill Decoration Among the
   Indians of N. America by W. C. Orchard (B00/01) $8.95
The Technique of North American Indian Beadwork
   by Monte Smith (B00/02) $10.95
Techniques of Beading Earrings
   by Deon DeLange (B00/03) $8.95
More Techniques of Beading Earrings
   by Deon DeLange (B00/04) $8.95
America's *First* First World War: The French
   and Indian War by Tim Todish (B00/05) $8.95
Crow Indian Beadwork by Wildschut & Ewers (B00/06) $8.95
New Adventures in Beading Earrings
   by Laura Reid (B00/07) $8.95
North American Indian Burial Customs
   by Dr. H. C. Yarrow (B00/09) $9.95
Traditional Indian Crafts
   by Monte Smith (B00/10) $9.95
Traditional Indian Bead and Leather Crafts
   by M. Smith & M. VanSickle (B00/11) $9.95
Indian Clothing of the Great Lakes: 1740-1840
   by Sheryl Hartman (B00/12) $10.95
Shinin' Trails: A Possibles Bag of Fur Trade Trivia
   by John Legg (B00/13) $7.95
Adventures in Creating Earrings by L. Reid (B00/14) $9.95
A Circle of Power by William Higbie (B00/15) $7.95
Etienne Provost: Man of the Mountains
   by Jack Tykal (B00/16) $9.95
A Quillwork Companion by Jean Heinbuch (B00/17) $9.95
Making Indian Bows & Arrows ... The Old Way
   by Doug Wallentine (B00/18) $10.95
Making Arrows...The Old Way by Wallentine (B00/19) $4.00
Hair of the Bear: Campfire Yarns and Stories
   by Eric Bye (B00/20) $9.95
How to Tan Skins the Indian Way
   by Evard Gibby (B00/21) $4.50
A Beadwork Companion by Jean Heinbuch (B00/22) $10.95
Beads and Cabochons: How To Create Fashion Jewelry
   and Earrings by Patricia Lyman (B00/23) $9.95
Earring Designs by Sig: Book I
   by Sigrid Wynne-Evans (B00/24) $8.95
Creative Crafts by Marj by Marj Schneider (B00/25) $9.95

CLASSIC EARRING DESIGNS

by Nola May

No wonder beading is so popular! It is easy to learn and the results are both beautiful and personally satisfying. Author Nola May believes beaded earrings frame a person's face like a picture and highlight the personality within without saying a word.

It is easy to find just the right "frame" in this collection of designs, because the color combinations were inspired by mother nature herself. Here are the pinks, purples, and blues of sweet peas; the yellow, gold, cream, rust and burgundy tones of chrysanthemums; the reds, oranges and golds of maple trees in the fall; and much, much more.

Perfect for beginning and intermediate beaders, this book will also stimulate the creativity of advanced beaders. The introduction contains information on materials needed for beading and general instructions. Each section contains complete, easy-to-follow instructions, plenty of illustrations, and a variety of bead-by-bead patterns featuring the use of many different accent beads.

Basic Comanche Weave (also known as Brick Stitch) instructions are given, followed by Comanche Weave Variations which include Bugle Bead Tops, Bugle and Seed Bead Combinations, Seed Bead Base Rows, Tube Earrings, Stars, and Diamonds. The last section presents beautiful Round and Rectangular Bead Lace Earrings.

There are 52 original patterns and 8 color plates which show 32 designs plus the three shown in full color on the cover.

This is a book every crafter will want to own and use, again and again!